CITY C~~YCLING~~
MILAN

Rapha.

✿ **Thames & Hudson**

Created by Andrew Edwards and Max Leonard of
Tandem London, a design, print and editorial studio

Thanks to Riccardo Guasco for illustrations;
Antonio Colombo, Alessandra Cusatelli, Fabrizio
Aghito, Paolo Erzegovesi and Miriam Mosetti of
Gruppo; and Angelo Giangregorio

First published in the United Kingdom in 2013 by
Thames & Hudson Ltd, 181A High Holborn, London WC1V 7QX

City Cycling Milan © 2013 Andrew Edwards and Max Leonard
Illustrations © 2013 Thames & Hudson Ltd, London and Rapha Racing Ltd

Designed by Andrew Edwards

Illustrations by Riccardo Guasco, riccardoguasco.com

All Rights Reserved. No part of this publication may be reproduced
or transmitted in any form or by any means, electronic or mechanical,
including photocopy, recording or any other information storage and
retrieval system, without prior permission in writing from the publisher.

British Library Cataloguing-in-Publication Data
A catalogue record for this book is available from the British Library

ISBN 978-0-500-29107-8

Printed and bound in China by Everbest Printing Co Ltd

To find out about all our publications, please visit
www.thamesandhudson.com. There you can subscribe
to our e-newsletter, browse or download our current catalogue,
and buy any titles that are in print.

CONTENTS

HOW TO USE THIS GUIDE

This Milan volume of the City Cycling series is designed to give you the confidence to explore the city by bike at your own pace. On the front flaps is a locator map of the whole city to help you orient yourself. We've divided the city up into four different neighbourhoods: Centro Storico (p. 10); Brera (p. 16); Zona Tortona and Navigli (p. 22); and Isola and Porta Venezia (p. 28). All are easily accessible by bike, and are full of cafés, bars, galleries, museums, shops and parks. Each area is mapped in detail, and our recommendations for places of interest and where to fuel up on coffee and cake, as well as where to find a Wi-Fi connection, are marked. Take a pootle round on your bike and see what suits you.

The neighbourhood maps also show bike routes, bike shops and landmarks – everything you need to navigate safely and pinpoint specific locations across a large section of the centre of town. If you fancy a set itinerary, turn to A Day On The Bike, also on the front flaps. It takes you on a relaxed 25km (16-mile) route through some of the parts of Milan we haven't featured in the neighbourhood sections. Pick and choose the bits you fancy, go from back to front, and use the route as it suits you.

A section on Racing and Training (p. 34) fills you in on some of Milan's cycling heritage and provides ideas for longer rides if you want to explore the beautiful countryside around the city, while Essential Bike Info (p. 38) discusses road etiquette and the ins and outs of navigating your way along Milan's roads and cycle routes. Finally, Links and Addresses (p. 42) will give you the practical details you need to know.

MILAN: THE CYCLING CITY

Elegant lines, classic materials and timeless style… Milanese bicycles – and their riders – do live up to the city's reputation as one of the fashion capitals of the world. Like the fashion, Milan is understated and restrained, grown up – even slightly buttoned up – yet with a calm self assurance. If you're used to Rome or the south of Italy, you might even find it austere. But come during one of the many fashion weeks (men's in January and June, women's in February and September) or, even better, in April during the multidisciplinary furniture and design festival that is the Salone del Mobile, and you'll see another side. They're some of the best times to visit, with many events in the industrial spaces of the Zona Tortona, one of our featured neighbourhoods (p. 22). Visitors at other times of the year won't be disappointed: there are enough galleries, openings and events to keep even the most avid culture vulture happy.

Whether you're there for an event, in the spring and summer sun or misty autumn (the city can get quite cold, especially in January and February), Milan by bike is a surprising and frequently enchanting experience. The city centre is compact and pretty, packed with historic buildings and world-class art institutions. Outside the core, the neighbourhoods of large bourgeois residences, the former industrial areas that fuelled Milan's prosperity and the inner-city developments resulting from Italy's postwar 'economic miracle' are fun to explore, and cyclists need not feel intimidated. In contrast to other Italian cities, bike use in Milan is on the up, and, although Italian drivers have a reputation for being erratic, inside the city they are reasonably courteous and aware of cyclists.

Milan used to suffer from a big traffic problem. In the 2000s, it had the second-highest rate of car ownership in Europe (behind Rome), and was notorious for its smog. In 2008, the city's first woman mayor, Letizia Moratti, introduced an emissions charge on old, polluting vehicles in the city centre, but when that didn't improve the situation, she introduced Area C, a congestion charge on all vehicles in the central area, four years later. While many motorists and shopkeepers have complained – and it remains controversial – it has contributed to a large drop in vehicle numbers (over a third fewer entered in a check three months afterwards, although the number has since crept up), better air quality and a better environment for cyclists. A blanket 30kph (19mph) city-centre speed limit also helps.

The city council, too, is promoting cycling, and their BikeMi cycle-sharing scheme has been a great success, with daily use of the fun and convenient yellow bikes peaking at around 12,000 journeys. There's also a commitment to more bikes and docking stations, and to widen the scheme further into the suburbs. The city is investing in new bike parking spaces and bike lanes, with 100km (62 miles) due to be added to the existing 140km (87 miles) by 2015. That's when Milan plays host to the World Expo, the first Universal Exposition since 2010. Its theme is 'Feeding the Planet, Energy for Life'; green sustainable urban transport, therefore, is perfectly in tune with the city's aims. In the run-up to the Expo, a new 'Via d'Acqua' bike path connecting the Naviglio Grande canal with the Rho and Fiera exhibition areas, will be constructed, along with new bike lanes in the very centre of town. For more on important bike safety pointers, city riding tips and an explanation of how to use BikeMi, turn to Essential Bike Info (p. 38).

Visitors to the city might also look to how Milaneses ride their bikes for pointers – elegantly and fearlessly over the cobbles and the uneven paving slabs of the historic centre, talking non-stop on their phones, carrying umbrellas to keep their overcoats dry or nonchalantly on pavements. There's an emerging cohort of 'urban' bikers, fixed-wheel riders and bicycle-polo players who frequent the several cycle boutiques and Milan's first bicycle café, Upcycle (p. 30), but overall there's a strong and abiding bike culture in the town, perhaps due to the many famous bicycle companies who have made bikes in the area since the very start of the bicycle era (for more see the Racing and Training section; p. 34).

You'll see every shade of Milanese riding to and from work, or to their favourite lunch spot. Get on your bike and join them.

NEIGHBOURHOODS

CENTRO STORICO
CULTURE, ARCHITECTURE, SIGHTS

Where else can we start in Milan but in the <u>Piazza del Duomo</u>, in front of the **Duomo** ① itself? Construction started in 1386 and continued for centuries: Napoleon ordered the French state to loan the money for the front façade in 1805, and the final gate was finished in the 1960s. The piazza is surrounded by treasures, including the **Museo del Novecento** ②, positioned in a suitably modern setting behind the classical façade of the Palazzo dell'Arengario. Next door is the **Palazzo Reale** ③, the former seat of Milan's government, which now hosts cultural events. Nearby, keep your eyes peeled for the sculptures of *El Bissun* on the **Palazzo Arcivescovile** ④, the serpent

eating a man that is a symbol of the city. It was once the heraldic emblem of the Visconti family, and is now seen on Inter Milan shirts and Alfa Romeo cars, and on an earlier incarnation of the Cinelli bicycle head badges.

Cycling is slow going on the roads near the Duomo, and the huge pavement slabs can be uncomfortable on skinny-tyred bikes (many of the elegant town bikes have chunky tyres to deal with this), so take care if you're heading to the **Biblioteca Ambrosiana** ⑤, where more art treasures lie, with paintings by Titian, Brueghel and Caravaggio, as well as works by Leonardo da Vinci. Opposite is the little known **Museo Mangini Bonomi** ⑥, a collection of curios including wooden horses, clocks, suits of armour and a mechanical monkey smoking a cigarette, all ranged around a private courtyard.

The nearby <u>Piazza dei Mercanti</u> is where the Critical Mass bicycle rally meets on the last Friday of every month; if you don't fancy that, head north from the Piazza del Duomo and push your bike through the **Galleria Vittorio Emanuele II** ⑦, the grandest, most beautiful shopping mall you'll ever see. On the other side is **La Scala** ⑧, the iconic opera house, and **Trussardi alla Scala** ⑨, where Milan's high society meets for a quick espresso and people-watching in the beautiful square. For a more relaxed drink or a bite to eat, **Pasticceria Marchesi** ⑩ is one of the city's most famous pastry shops and little altered since the nineteenth century. **Grom** ⑪, meanwhile, is one of Milan's best *gelaterias*, and foodies shouldn't miss **Rinascente** ⑫. The department store has a juice bar and a rooftop café, while in the basement the Rinascente Design Supermarket showcases more than two hundred international furniture, homeware and lighting design brands, as well as having its own café.

Other interesting shopping experiences to be found in the city centre include **Hoepli** ⑬, a labyrinthine bookshop, and **New Old**

Camera ⑭, a vintage camera shop in the tight back streets behind the <u>Via Broletto</u>. **Wait and See** ⑮ is a womenswear boutique away from the 'Golden Quad' of fashion streets near Montenapoleone metro station. Run by an ex-design consultant of Missoni, it takes advantage of the distance from the established fashion houses to present a fresher, more contemporary selection. For men, there's **Berluti** ⑯, a renowned boot-maker that makes traditional shoes and leather goods. Afterwards, head to the **Hotel Straf** ⑰, where the minimalist bar and its carefully selected designer furniture hosts a cool crowd at *aperitivo* hour, and show off your purchases.

REFUELLING

FOOD

Peck ⑱ bills itself as an 'Italian Temple of Gastronomical Delights' – and doesn't disappoint

Luini ⑲ is a well-known *panzerotto* joint, serving hot doughy pockets of tomato and cheese, or chocolate

DRINK

Caffè Zucca ⑳: stand at the same bar where Verdi once stood for an espresso

Gin Rosa ㉑ is a *pasticceria* that turns into Milan's must-see *aperitivo* place after hours

WI-FI

Go to **Arnold Coffee** ㉒ for the free Wi-Fi – but not for the coffee!

VIA MELONE
VIA DELL'ORSO
VIA ARIGO BOITO
RIENNALE
VIA CUSANI
VIA DEL LAURO
Y
M CAIROLI
VIA ROVELLO
VIA DEL BOSSI
VIA SAN TOMASO
14
VIA CLERICI
VIA SAN GIOVANNI SUL MURO
VIA MANFREDO CAMPERIO
VIA PORLEZZA
VIA BROLETTO
VIA SAN PRO
VIA MERAVIGLI
VIA TOMMASO GROSSI
M CORDUSIO
10
VIA SANTA MARIA FULCORINA
VIA GAETANO NEGRI
VIA OREFICI
VIA BERNARDINO LUINI
VIA ANSPERTO
22
VIA ARMORARI
VIA DELLA POSTA
VIA MORIGI
VIA VIGNA
VIA BOCCHETTO
VIA DEL BOLLO
18
VIA BORROMEI
VIA DELLA SPADINA
6
5
VIA CAPPUCCIO
VIA MORIGI
VIA DEL BOLLO
VIA DELLE ASOLE
VIA SANT'ORSOLA
VIA TORINO
VIA SAN MAURILIO
VIA LUPETTA
15
VIA NERINO
VIA CIRCO
VIA SANTA MARTA
VIA DELLA PALLA
VIA CAPPUCCIO
VIA BAGNERA
VIA DEI PIATTI
VIA MEDICI
VIA AMEDEI
VIA FIENO
VIA SONCINO
VIA STAMPA
VIA CESARE CORRENTI
VIA SAN VITO
PIAZZA

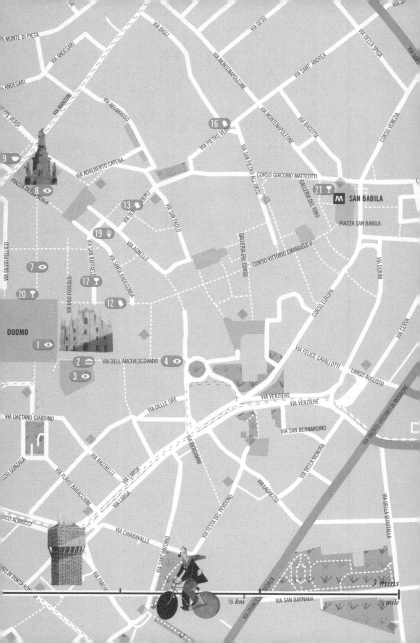

BRERA

SMART BARS, PRIVATE GALLERIES AND SHOPPING

Brera began its life as a neighbourhood stuck between Milan's old Roman and medieval walls. At its heart is the <u>Via Brera</u>, which lies immediately north of the Duomo (p. 10) in the *centro storico*, west of the **Giardini Indro Montanelli** ① and east of the Sempione and Castello Sforzesco. During the Renaissance, it became a hive of artistic activity, and has attracted poets, artists and writers ever since. Renowned as a bohemian hang-out, its imposing buildings, immaculate pavements and cobbled streets mean that it's now more of a tourist trap, but there's plenty here to see – not least the clothing

establishments on the Via Brera itself, all brown cashmere scarves, dark leather shoes and quintessentially Milanese style. Check out **Massimo Alba** ② for a relaxed, modern take on the look. Once you've had your fill of window shopping, and peeked into the tantalizingly closed courtyards that line the street, head to the **Pinacoteca di Brera** ③, housed in a fourteenth-century convent, which since 1776 has contained a growing, now world-renowned art collection on a par with the Louvre or the Prado, majoring in the Italian masters. There's also an astronomical museum, which often gets forgotten but is very good. Something of a contemporary counterpart, though not of the same stature, is **Padiglione d'Arte Contemporanea** ④, better known as **PAC**, a vast, Ignazio Gardella-designed space dedicated to the display and research of contemporary art.

Cycle north of the Pinacoteca, and Via Brera opens out and becomes lined with bars and restaurants. Take a left and you'll find yourself in the <u>Via Fiori Chiari</u>, the destination for a cluster of chic, carefully curated vintage design and furniture shops, including

Il Cirmolo ⑤, each with its own speciality and full of antiques, industrial salvage and objets d'art. Or squeeze your bike through the little alleys to the west, and you'll emerge from behind the stunning **Santa Maria del Carmine** ⑥ into a picturesque square. <u>Via Mercato</u> in front of the church is pleasant enough, but follow it north to the <u>Corso Giuseppe Garibaldi</u>, the area's best and liveliest street for *aperitivi*. Sit at one of the bars and watch Milan's finest chat, mingle and drink after work. Nearby is **Rossignoli** ⑦, a fine old bike shop, and purveyor of the many beautiful Rossignoli ('nightingale') bikes you'll see around the city. Milanese people obviously care for them, as you'll see elegant bicycles of all vintages in use in the streets.

Head north again, and you'll enter gallery territory. Antonio Colombo, head of the Cinelli bicycle and Columbus tubing businesses, runs **Antonio Colombo Arte Contemporanea** ⑧ in the <u>Via Solferino</u>, specializing in work inspired by street art and comics. Nearby **Galleria Blu** ⑨ was founded in 1957 and is one of the most prestigious in Milan, having exhibited Braque, Kandinsky and

Giacometti, among others. **Cardi Black Box** ⑩ is comparatively new on the block, but has an international list.

There's a healthy representation of classic Italian design in the area, too. **Kartell** ⑪, the Milan-based company that's made innovative plastic furniture since 1949, has a flagship store here (there's also the Kartell Museum, out of town in the hills), and **Guzzini** ⑫, the kitchenware design firm, is also represented. **Galleria Colombari** ⑬ displays classic twentieth-century international design. For a glimpse into how it would feel to live among such objects, visit the **Villa Necchi Campiglio** ⑭. Located in the so-called 'silent quarter', full of large bourgeois residences, the Piero Portaluppi-designed house is as if frozen in time from the 1930s, with original furniture and two valuable art bequests adorning the walls. It featured in the Italian art-house film *I Am Love*, starring Tilda Swinton.

REFUELLING

FOOD	DRINK
Ham Holy Burger ⑮ uses lean beef from rare-breed cattle to cook up its gourmet burgers	Radetzky ⑯ is at the centre of Brera's street socializing
	Biancolatte ⑰ for good coffee

WI-FI
Obikà Mozarella Bar ⑱ has delicious cheeses and also Wi-Fi

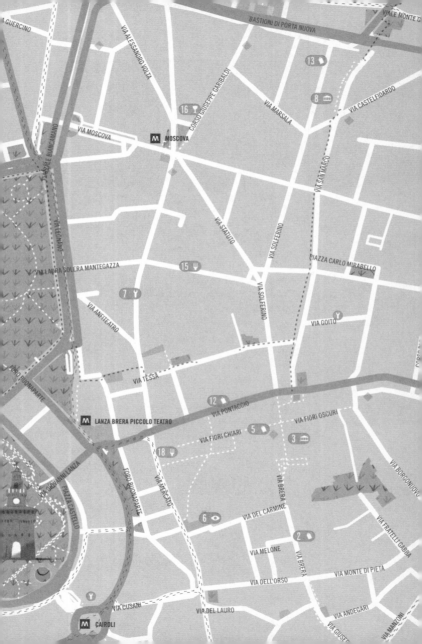

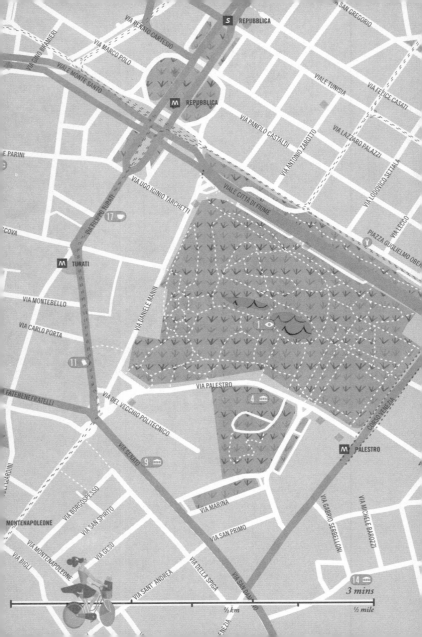

ZONA TORTONA & NAVIGLI

DESIGN, FASHION HAPPENINGS AND NIGHTLIFE

Defined by the sweeping curve of railway tracks and arrow-straight canals, this neighbourhood in southwest Milan takes in the liveliest and most dynamic areas in the city, as well as some of the area around the Porta Ticinese, closer to the city centre. Approaching from the northeast, you'll cycle past the grand Roman columns and quiet **Piazza San Lorenzo** ①, as well as **Basilica di Sant'Eustorgio** ②, with its peaceful park, and the restored medieval city gate, **Porta Ticinese** ③. They're reminders of Milan's long history, but the main reason people come this way is for the new and exciting: <u>Corso di Porta Ticinese</u> is a happening street, and Piazza San Lorenzo an important stopping-off point for local nightlife. **Serendeepity** ④, a dance record shop, might get you in the mood, as will **Birdland** ⑤, a specialist jazz record and music shop.

From San Lorenzo, cycle down the <u>Naviglio Grande</u>; the cycle path on the right-hand side extends a long way out of town (see A Day On The Bike to explore further). Taking place on the quayside on the last Sunday of each month is the **Mercatone del Naviglio Grande** ⑥, one of Europe's great antiques markets, selling furniture, salvage, books, jewelry, and more. Since many Italians don't care for pre-owned things, there are some great bargains to be found. Among the touristy restaurants you'll also find **Libraccio** ⑦, a bookshop packed to the rafters with guides and interesting second-hand books, and, on the <u>Naviglio Pavese</u>, nightlife that gets going later: **Sacrestia Farmacia Alcolica** ⑧ is one of the more popular and salubrious options. It's very close to **Dodici Cicli** ⑨, home of the Milanese urban bike brand, which stocks a host of cool bespoke bits for your bicycle.

Before you head into the Zona Tortona, don't miss **Forma** ⑩, a photography centre with an emphasis on historic and fashion photos, housed in a former tram shed. To get to Tortona, take the beautiful iron staircase behind Porta Genova station, or, if your bike's too heavy, head north to Via Savona. Tortona, a former industrial and working quarter, is somewhat trapped – or protected – by the railway. Its narrow streets are flanked by high residential blocks and warehouses, and today it's home to studios, art spaces and, increasingly, to the big fashion houses, including the **Armani HQ** ⑪, in an old Nestlé factory. Also using the vast, hangar-like spaces are the **Fondazione Arnaldo Pomodoro** ⑫, an arts foundation in an old turbine factory, and the **Spazio Ex Ansaldo** ⑬, renovated by David Chipperfield Architects to make a 'City of Culture'. **Superstudio** ⑭, a complex of buildings in a former bicycle factory, hosts design exhibitions and studio space, and is frequently used as a runway venue during fashion week; pop in to the **Superstudio Café** ⑮ to see who you can spot. **Galvanotecnica Bugatti** ⑯, meanwhile, holds exhibitions, pop-ups and temporary events around an inviting courtyard.

During the Salone del Mobile, Zona Tortona, where many of the Salone's fringe events take place, becomes one big street party – and it's quite an experience. During the rest of the year, the streets are quieter but still full of interest: <u>Via Savona</u> and <u>Via Tortona</u> are the main drags. Two good shopping destinations are **D Magazine** ⑰, a designer outlet, and **Armadio di Laura** ⑱ for vintage finds, where you just might find some photoshoot cast-offs from Milan's fashionistas, while **Home Made** ⑲ and traditional trattoria **Ristorante Boccino** ⑳ are where to go for delicious food. To take the weight off your feet, try the **DesignLibraryCafé** ㉑, which extends the DesignLibrary's mission of creating a welcoming environment for research, study or just talk about design. **Gogol & Company** ㉒, meanwhile, is a relaxed bookshop, literary café and exhibition space.

REFUELLING

FOOD

Angelo's Bistrot ㉓ for homely dining in a cool interior with 1960s design pieces

Fabbrica Pizza con Cucina ㉔: good pizza and fast, friendly service

DRINK

Morna ㉕ is an old-fashioned bar overlooking a *bocce* (traditional bowls) court

WI-FI

California Bakery ㉖ ㉗ (Piazza Sant'Eustorgio and Via Tortona) offers American-style baked treats while you check your emails

ISOLA & PORTA VENEZIA

MILAN'S BOHEMIAN SIDE

Isola, the 'island' in the north of Milan, is cut off from the rest of town by a spaghetti junction of railway lines – the Porta Garibaldi station to the south is busier with local trains and daily commuters than the impressive, imposing marble **Stazione di Milano Centrale** ① nearby. As such, Isola has remained somewhat underdeveloped and anachronistic, scruffier and more bohemian than some parts of Milan, but distinctive and independent – a formerly working-class industrial area with many small shops, galleries, ateliers and artists studios. As well as Isola, this neighbourhood guide also journeys around the Porta Venezia area.

If you're travelling from the centre of town, you'll probably cycle up past **10 Corso Como** ②, an essential stop. Around the shady green courtyard café is a bazaar of books, design and fashion, as well as a photography gallery, all curated by Carla Sozzani, a former *Vogue* editor and writer. (**Books Import** ③, to the east, also has a brilliant selection of international art, architecture and design books.) At the end of Corso Como is the Porta Nuova development, all gleaming skyscrapers, including the curved Unicredit building, at 231m (758 ft) the tallest in Italy. Eventually, the development will house MOdAM, a fashion school and museum, though the completion dates are unclear. For now, it's best to navigate around the edge of the building site, taking the road to the west over the railway lines into Isola.

<u>Piazzale Lagosta</u> is at the centre of the neighbourhood, and is surrounded by quirky little shops and cafés, including **MiCamera** ④, Milan's best shop for new and vintage cameras, and **Chiedi Alla**

Polvere ⑤, a retro furniture showroom with pieces from the 1950s to the '70s. **Galleria MK** ⑥ also has vintage furniture design, and is slightly more restrained, while **Brand New Gallery** ⑦ is one of the more established contemporary art galleries in the neighbourhood. **L'Isa** ⑧ is a locally focused space – a home for crafts, accessories and jewelry, where you can meet the artisans behind the products at the Wednesday open evenings. If you want to meet Isola's locals outside the shops and galleries, the best place to go is **Frida** ⑨, a laid-back and sprawling bar in a former industrial space, or, for bike help, **Ciclofficina Stecca** ⑩, an open bike workshop that welcomes cyclists on Wednesdays and Saturdays.

The real destination for bike fans, however, is **Upcycle** ⑪, Milan's first bicycle café, a spacious venue that also hosts bike-themed events. To get there from Isola, head towards the **Pirelli Tower** ⑫, Italy's first skyscraper, which was built for the Pirelli tyre corporation. The company has since moved, and its former factories in the northern suburbs are now renowned as giant exhibition spaces, which special-ize in site-specific installations. The **HangarBicocca** ⑬, as they are known, are about 3km (2 miles) off-map, but well worth a ride out: cycle out of Isola up the <u>Via Arbe</u> and keep heading straight to the Via Chiese. The Hangar will be on your right; you'll see its round

tower from a distance to guide you in. Also significant is the Zona Lambrate, near Upcycle, where several galleries, notably **Galleria Francesca Minini** ⑭ and **Galleria Massimo De Carlo** ⑮, are clustered in a former industrial area.

For evening entertainment, the area around the **Porta Venezia Metro** ⑯ is popular with locals. We recommend **Bar Basso** ⑰, an old-school favourite that claims to have invented the *Negroni sbagliato* (Negroni with Prosecco). **ATM Bobino** ⑱ to the west is a minimal bar that is also typically Milanese, while for jazz lovers the **Blue Note** ⑲ established its first European venue in Isola. It has two shows a night, the first sitting being a supper club.

REFUELLING

FOOD	DRINK
Ungaro 1956 ⑳ is a favourite *pasticceria*	**NordEst Caffè** ㉒ is an authentic coffee stop
Blu Milano ㉑ for a more contemporary lunch	**Cantine Isola** ㉓ for an unrivalled selection of wines, and good nibbles too

WI-FI
Pavé ㉔ is a shabby-chic café/bakery with great sandwiches, coffee and free Internet

RACING AND TRAINING

Many parts of cycling-mad Italy could convincingly make a claim to be the home of Italian cycling – Tuscany and its hills, where many pros live and train; the Dolomites, where the greatest battles of the Giro d'Italia are fought; Liguria, the birthplace of Costante Girardengo – but Milan and the surrounding region are surely its heart. Lombardia has hundreds of cycling clubs and amateur races, and thousands of riders annually make the pilgrimage to the cyclists' chapel, Madonna del Ghisallo, high above the shores of Lake Como, around 70km (43 miles) from Milan. Filled with champions' bicycles and jerseys, it stands next to the **Museo del Ciclismo Madonna del Ghisallo**, equally full of memorabilia.

Each year, the **Giro di Lombardia** (now known simply as Il Lombardia), won by Fausto Coppi five times, climbs the steep slopes from picture-postcard lakeside towns like Bellagio, past the chapel; on the morning of the race, a special mass is held. When Il Lombardia was founded in 1905, it started and finished in Milan, and, though it has since visited many towns in the region, it still occasionally returns, before wending its way up to the Alpine foothills around Como. Races aside, the history, heritage and fantastic hills make the area a popular weekend destination for Milan's cyclists. An amateur Gran Fondo event is often run alongside the Lombardia, though this did not take place in 2013. There's also a Gran Fondo for Milan's other great one-day Classic, the **Milano–Sanremo**, the first Monument of the cycling season. Run in mid-March, it takes riders from the wintry gloom of the Lombardy plains over the Turchino pass to the spring sunshine of the Italian Riviera. At a shade under 300km (186 miles), it's the longest one-day race in the calendar (although in 2013, in the worst conditions seen since 1920, it was shortened as buses took riders from one side of the snow-bound Turchino to the other). Coppi's three wins are dwarfed by Eddy Merckx's seven; it was one of his favourite races.

Elsewhere in the region, there are many Gran Fondos for amateur riders to choose from, including the **Granfondo Colnago Desenzano** and **Felice Gimondi**, near Bergamo. And for the pros, the Milano-Torino semi-Classic one-day race, the oldest on the calendar, was reinstated in 2012 after a few years' absence – Alberto Contador won. Then there is, of course, the **Giro d'Italia**, which traditionally (but not always) finishes in Milan for a podium ceremony in the Piazza del Duomo. In 2011, the 150th edition, the final stage was an individual time trial that entered the city from the northwest, skirted the Parc Sempione and the Castello Sforzesco, before heading for the Duomo (p. 10). That year, Contador was triumphant; in 2012, which had a similar time trial, it was the Canadian Ryder Hesjedal, and in 2013 the race took a rare break from Milan to finish in Brescia.

Milan is famous in cycling for more than just races, however. The factories that fill the plains outside the city have intimately bound it to bicycle production. **Columbus**, the classic bicycle tubing manufacturer (which now, under Antonio Colombo, also owns **Cinelli**; see p. 18), is based a short drive outside, as is **Trafiltubi**, a steel supplier, and **Dedacciai**, which makes tubes, handlebars and other parts, isn't far away. As for bicycle makers, some of the most famous names in Italy come from Milan. **Bianchi**, now in Treviglio, first made its famous 'celeste'-coloured frames in <u>Via Nirone</u>; Cino Cinelli, when he retired from racing (he won the Milano–Sanremo in 1943), opened his factory in <u>Via Egidio Folli</u>. **Olmo** still exists in the Ticinese neighbourhood, while **De Rosa** and **Casati** are in nearby towns. Legnano bikes were made in the town of Legnano, while **Colnago**, the company of the legendary Ernesto Colnago, is based in Cambiago. Finally, Faliero 'The Tailor' Masi's frame-making firm was based in the **Vigorelli velodrome**, where his son still keeps a shop. For more on the Vigorelli, site of many hour-record attempts and track records, check our Day On The Bike section on the front flaps.

Sadly, Vigorelli has been closed for many years, and the closest there is now to inner-city track racing is the **Red Hook Criterium Milano**, a track-bike race through closed city streets, which attracts some of the best 'urban' riders from across the world. It used to be on the same weekend (the second in October) as the Lombardia, making a fantastic double bill, but since the Lombardia is now run a week or two earlier, you'll have to fill the time in between with cycling. **Esposito Massimo** is a good bike shop for road-bike spares or repairs, as are Olmo and **Rossignoli** (p. 18). For a slow, friendly club ride, try riding with the **Genova 1913** cycle club, or for a fast ride out of town,

riders meet in Monza – about 10km (6 miles) north of Milan, outside the Villa Reale di Monza, leaving at 9am in winter and half an hour earlier in spring and summer. After your ride, head to Milan's bicycle café **Upcycle** (p. 30) for a recovery espresso. For all contact information, head to the Links and Addresses section.

ESSENTIAL BIKE INFO

For some, the idea of cycling in Italian traffic is intimidating, but in Milan, at least, these fears are mostly unfounded. Drivers are quite courteous, speeds are relatively low – there's a 30kph (19mph) speed limit in force across most of the city centre – and congestion levels are dropping thanks to a congestion charge. Here are some more tips for hassle-free cycling in Milan:

ETIQUETTE

Cycling in Milan can seem hectic or chaotic, but drivers are tolerant and other cyclists are friendly. Take note to keep rolling smoothly:
- Everybody is very accepting of unorthodox actions
- Milanese traffic keeps on moving – cars keep on driving, pedestrians walk, bikes pedal – until something moves into its path. At that point, it cedes and lets the person through, whatever they might be travelling on
- Don't be foolhardy, but don't be reticent either. Be purposeful in your actions and drivers will understand what you're doing and let you do it
- The flip side is to be tolerant, and aware, of what others are up to
- Signalling when manoeuvring is a good idea
- Cyclists pay little mind to many rules of the road – cycling across piazzas, up pavements, through red lights. If you decide to do this, be slow and careful, and courteous to pedestrians

SAFETY

The etiquette tips above are useful, but here are a few more pointers:
- Milan isn't known for its cobbles like Belgium is, but it has some very rough road surfaces, including broken tarmac and large paving slabs, often with big gaps in between them. Make sure you watch where your front wheel is headed
- Watch out for trams – and tramlines too, which can catch a tyre and become treacherously slippery in the wet

- Because the roads are quite narrow and busy, left turns can be difficult, especially when you're not quite sure of where you're going. Remember that if you're at all in doubt, it's better to pull in and wait for the traffic to pass, or to cross on foot

SECURITY

Milan doesn't seem quite as much of a thieves' paradise as some big cities, but common sense applies. Do not leave any bike unlocked and unattended, and take your cues from local cyclists: if you don't see any bikes locked in a certain area, it's probably not a good idea to leave yours there either. If you've brought a valuable bike to town, always lock it with a good lock to something immovable. Think about using two locks, so that opportunist bike thieves will pick an easier target.

FINDING YOUR WAY

Milan is easy to understand on a map: it used to be circled by canals, now mainly paved over with roads (except for those in the Navigli area). And, from the Duomo (p. 10), there are main roads fanning out, like spokes in a wheel, towards the many *porte*, the old city gates. These are useful to navigate by, and the inner ring roads (Viales Papiniano, d'Annunzio, Caldara, etc) is fine to ride around – though be careful on those left turns.

Aside from that, we advise keeping the map close, as the compact, twisty streets will soon have you confused. You'll find yourself hauling your bike up kerbs, cycling up one-way streets and on the pavement, but don't worry too much – everybody else does it, too.

CITY BIKES AND BIKE HIRE

The Milan city bike scheme, **BikeMi**, is a great success, and may be unique in that the bikes are shaft-driven – they have a metal rod to convey your power to the back wheel rather than a chain. Other than that, they're similar in design to the Parisian Vélibs, and are generally well maintained. Docking stations are spaced around 300m (984 ft) or so apart, the scheme is open for use from 7am until 2am every day, and hours are extended for some special events, such as fashion week. The boundaries of the scheme are being extended outwards, and you should be covered wherever you want to go.

Annual membership costs €36, and for that you get your own card. As a visitor, you'll probably want daily or weekly hire at €2.50 or €6, respectively. Register on the Internet for your user ID and PIN, which you enter on the docking station terminals. Either way, you get unlimited bike hires, and the first half hour is free; after that, you'll be charged 50¢ for each subsequent half hour. You must return the bike within two hours as the scheme is designed for short hops, to keep the bikes in circulation. If you keep it longer than two hours, the fines are only in multiples of €2, but you'll find yourself blocked if you break the rules too many times. In reality, only the longest of cross-town trips will take more than half an hour, so you should be OK, although you may want to secure your bike with the supplied cable lock if you're popping into a shop, or sitting down for an espresso.

If you'd prefer to hire a normal town bike, **AWS Bici** is the place to go. And, for a road bike, **Esposito Massimo** (p. 36) has a small stock.

OTHER PUBLIC TRANSPORT

Bikes are not allowed on Milanese trams, except on the Milano–Limbiate Hospital and the Milano–Cusano–Desio lines, on which each person is allowed one bike. It costs €1, and it must be carried on board via the rear doors. Similarly, on the Metro, you're allowed to take a bike for a €1 fee (this applies to bikes in bags, too), but the hours are very specific: on normal working days, it's only from 8pm until close; on weekends and public holidays, and during the whole month of August, bikes are allowed any time; in December, they're not allowed at all. Find the carriage with the bicycle symbol on the window: that's the one for you.

On suburban and regional trains that display a bike symbol on the timetable, you must pay €3.50 for a bike ticket. This allows you multiple journeys within a 24-hour period (and bikes in bags go free). Ferrovie dello Stato trains impose no time restrictions; on LeNORD trains, they're only allowed between 10am and 4pm, and after 8pm.

TRAVELLING TO MILAN WITH BIKES

Trains are the safest way to travel with a bike. Italian national trains allow bikes for €5, and international trains for a €12 fee. Bikes in bags can be taken free of charge. For international services, there are a few direct TGVs from Paris each day, which take bagged bicycles for free. The large luggage racks mean the whole business is fairly hassle-free, and two strategies seem to work: either race to the front of the queue, so that you can be sure of securing the space you want in the rack; or, if your bike bag is fairly slimline, wait until everyone else has stowed their luggage, and slide it in on top.

Unfortunately, if you're travelling from Britain, from 2013 Eurostar will not allow a bagged bike as normal carry-on luggage. The maximum baggage dimensions are 85 × 85cm (33 × 33 in.), which rules out all but folding bikes. Since you'll be connecting to other trains, it's best to put your bike in a bag, 120cm (47 in.) maximum length, and send it via Eurostar's registered baggage service. The 'Turn Up and Go' option, where you leave it at a counter in the check-in hall, costs £10 each way. Make sure you arrive in good time to the station: the registered baggage counter is quite a walk from the passenger terminal. It's possible these regulations will change, so do check the website for the most up-to-date information.

The other best train route to Milan is from Germany, via Munich. Like the Eurostar, German high-speed ICE trains will not allow bike bags bigger than 85cm (33 in.) in any dimension. Slower Intercity and Eurocity (IC and EC) trains allow bikes to be wheeled on board if you pay for a reservation, or bikes in bags for free, so it's best to factor in a non high-speed train if you're travelling to Milan from Germany. Lastly, perhaps the most romantic option is the slow train through the Alps, via the Gotthard Pass from Zurich. Most Swiss trains allow bicycles, for a fee, unless it is indicated to the contrary on the timetable. Bikes in bags are fine. All Milan's airports are a long way from the city centre, and stuck in a spaghetti junction of major, traffic-filled roads, so cycling to and from your flight is not advised. Take public transport into town instead.

LINKS AND ADDRESSES

10 Corso Como
Corso Como, 10, 20154
10corsocomo.com

Angelo's Bistrot
Via Savona, 55, 20144

Antonio Colombo Arte Contemporanea
Via Solferino, 44, 20121
colomboarte.com

Armadio di Laura
Via Voghera, 25, 20144
armadiodilaura.it

Armani HQ
Via Ambrogio da Fossano
Bergognone, 59, 2014
armani.com

Arnold Coffee
Via Orefici, 26, 20123
arnoldcoffee.it

ATM Bobino
Bastioni di Porta Volta, 18/a, 20121
atmbobino.it

Bar Basso
Via Plinio, 39, 20129
barbasso.com

Bar della Crocetta
Corso di Porta Romana, 67, 20122

Bardelli
Corso Magenta, 13, 20123
mbardelli.com

Bar Magenta
Via Giosué Carducci, 13, 20123

Basilica di Sant'Eustorgio
Piazza Sant'Eustorgio, 1, 20123
santeustorgio.it

Berluti
Via Pietro Verri, 20121
berluti.com

Biancolatte
Via Filippo Turati, 30, 20121
biancolatte.it

Biblioteca Ambrosiana
Piazza Pio XI, 2, 20100
ambrosiana.it

Birdland
Via Cosimo del Fante, 16, 20122
birdlandjazz.it

Blue Note
Via Pietro Borsieri, 37, 20159
bluenotemilano.it

Blu Milano
Via Francesco Carmagnola, 5, 20159
blumilano.net

Books Import
Via Achille Maiocchi, 11, 20129
booksimport.it

Brand New Gallery
Via Carlo Farini, 32, 20159
brandnew-gallery.com

Caffè Zucca
Galleria Vittorio Emanuele II,
Piazza del Duomo, 20123
caffemiani.it

California Bakery
• Piazza Sant'Eustorgio, 4, 20122
• Via Tortona, 28, 20144
californiabakery.it

Cantine Isola
Via Paolo Sarpi, 30, 20154

Cardi Black Box
Corso di Porta Nuova, 38, 20121
cardiblackbox.com

Casa del Bianco
Corso Magenta, 2, 20123
casadelbiancomilano.it

Castello Sforzesco
Piazza Castello, 27029
milanocastello.it

Chiedi Alla Polvere
Via Cola Montano, 20159
chiediallapolvere.it

Design Library Café
Via Savona, 11, 20144
designlibrary.it

D Magazine
Via Forcella, 13, 20144
dmagazine.it

Duomo di Milano
Piazza del Duomo, 18, 20122
duomomilano.it

E. Marinella
Via Santa Maria alla Porta, 5, 20123
marinellanapoli.it

Erba Brusca
Alzaia Naviglio Pavese, 286, 20142
erbabrusca.it

Fabbrica Pizzeria con Cucina
Alzaia Naviglio Grande, 70, 20144

Fiera di Sinigaglia
Alzaia Naviglio Grande, 20100
fieradisinigaglia.it

Fleur Café
Corso Magenta, 48, 20123

Fondazione Arnaldo Pomodoro
Via Andrea Solari, 35, 20144
fondazionearnaldopomodoro.it

Forma
Piazza Tito Lucrezio Caro, 1, 20136
formafoto.it

Frida
Via Pollaiuolo, 3, 20159
fridaisola.it

Galleria Blu
Via Senato, 18, 20121
galleriablu.com

Galleria Colombari
Via Solferino, 37, 20121
galleriacolombari.com

Galleria Francesca Minini
Via Massimiano, 25, 20134
francescaminini.it

Galleria Massimo De Carlo
Via Privata Giovanni Ventura, 5, 20134
massimodecarlo.it

Galleria MK
Via Pietro Maroncelli, 2, 20154

Galleria Vittorio Emanuele II
Piazza del Duomo, 20123
visitamilano.it

Galvanotecnica Bugatti
Via Privata Gaspare Bugatti, 7, 20144
galvanotecnicabugatti.it

Gattullo Pasticceria
Piazzale di Porta Lodovica, 2, 20136
gattullo.it

Gelateria Toldo
Via Ponte Vetero, 9, 20121

Giardini Indro Montanelli
Corso Venezia, 55, 20129
comune.milano.it

Gin Rosa
Galleria San Babila, 4/b, 20122
gin-rosa.it

Gogol & Company
Via Savona, 101, 20144
gogolandcompany.com

Grom
Via Santa Margherita, 16, 20121
grom.it

Guzzini
Via Pontaccio 8/10, 20121
fratelliguzzini.com

Ham Holy Burger
Via Palermo, 15, 20121
hamholyburger.com

HangarBicocca
Via Privata Chiese, 2 20126
hangarbicocca.org

Hoepli
Via Ulrico Hoepli, 5, 20121
hoepli.it

Home Made
Via Tortona, 12, 20144
home-made.it

Hotel Straf
Via San Raffaele, 3, 20121
straf.it

Il Cirmolo
Via Fiori Chiari, 3, 20121
ilcirmoloantiquariato.it

Isola Della Moda
Via Francesco Carmagnola,
7, 20159
isoladellamoda.net

Kartell
Via Filippo Turati, 20121
kartell.it

La Scala
Via Filodrammatici, 2, 20121
teatroallascala.org

Libraccio
Via Corsico, 9, 20144
libraccio.it

Libreria degli Atellani
Via della Moscova, 28, 20121
atellani.it

L'Isa
Via della Pergola, 3, 20159

Luini
Via Santa Radegonda, 16, 20121
luini.it

Massimo Alba
Via Brera 8, 20121
massimoalba.com

**Mercatone del Naviglio
Grande**
Naviglio Grande, 20144
mercatonedellantiquariato.mi.it

MiCamera
Via Medardo Rosso, 19, 20159
micamera.com

Mom Café
Viale Montenero, 51, 20122

Morna
Via Tortona 21, Angolo Via
Gaspare Bugatti, 20144

Museo del Novecento
Piazza Duomo, 12, 20100
museodelnovecento.org

Museo Mangini Bonomi
Via dell'Ambrosiana, 20, 20123
museomanginibonomi.it

New Old Camera
Via Rovello, 5, 20121
newoldcamera.it

NordEst Caffè
Via Pietro Borsieri, 35, 20159

Obikà Mozzarella Bar
Via Santa Radegonda, 1, 20121
obika.com

**Padiglione d'Arte
Contemporanea**
Via Palestro, 14, 20121
comune.milano.it/pac

Palazzo Arcivescovile
Piazza Fontana, 2, 20122

Palazzo Reale
Piazza del Duomo, 12, 20100
comune.milano.it/palazzoreale

Pane e Acqua
Via Matteo Bandello, 14, 20123
paneacqua.com

Pasticceria Marchesi
Via Santa Maria alla Porta,
11, 20123
pasticceriamarchesi.it

Pavé
Via Felice Casati, 27, 20124
pavemilano.com

Peck
Via Spadari, 9, 20123
peck.it

Pinacoteca di Brera
Via Brera, 28, 20011
brera.beniculturali.it

Pirelli Tower
Piazza Duca D'Aosta, 20124

Radetzky
Corso Giuseppe Garibaldi,
105, 20124
radetzkycafe.com

Rinascente
Via Santa Radegonda, 3, 20121
rinascente.it

Ristorante Boccino
Via Tortona, 21, 20144
ristoranteboccino.it

Sacrestia Farmacia Alcolica
Via Conchetta, 20, 20136
sacrestia.com

Santa Maria del Carmine
Piazza del Carmine, 2, 20121
chiesadelcarmine.it

Santa Maria delle Grazie
Piazza Santa Maria delle
Grazie, 2, 20123
grazieop.it

Serendeepity
Corso di Porta Ticinese, 100,
20123
serendeepity.net

Spazio Ex Ansaldo
Via Tortona, 54, 20138

Spazio Rossana Orlandi
Via Matteo Bandello, 14–16,
20123
rossanaorlandi.com

Spontini
Via Gaspare Spontini, 4, 20131
pizzeriaspontini.it

**Studio Museo Achille
Castiglioni**
Piazza Castello, 27, 20121
achillecastiglioni.it

Superstudio + Café
Via Vincenzo Forcella, 13, 20144
superstudiogroup.com

Triennale di Milano
Viale Emilio Alemagna, 6,
20121
triennale.org

Trussardi alla Scala
Piazza della Scala, 5, 20121
trussardiallascala.com

Ungaro 1956
Via Carlo Ravizza, 23, 20149

Villa Necchi Campiglio
Via Wolfango Amedeo Mozart,
14, 20122
fondoambiente.it

Wait and See
Via Santa Marta, 14, 20123
waitandsee.it

BIKE SHOPS, CLUBS, RACES AND VENUES

For links to our racing and
training routes, please visit
citycyclingguides.com

AWS Bici
Via Ponte Seveso, 33, 20125
awsbici.com

Bianchi
Via delle Battaglie, 5,
24047 Treviglio
bianchi.com

BikeMi
bikemi.com

Casati
Via Camillo Prampolini, 7,
Monza 20900
ciclicasati.it

Ciclofficina Stecca
Via Gaetano de Castillia, 26,
20124

Cinelli
Via G. Di Vittorio, 21,
20090 Caleppio di Settala
cinelli.it

Colnago
Viale Brianza, 9,
20040 Cambiago
colnago.com

Columbus
Via G. Di Vittorio, 21,
20090 Caleppio di Settala
columbustubi.com

Dedacciai
Via L. Da Vinci, 19, 26010
Campagnola
dedacciai.com

De Rosa
Via Bellini, 24,
20095 Cusano Milanino
derosanews.com

Dodici Cicli
Via Conchetta, 17, 20136
dodicicicli.com

Esposito Massimo
Via Marco D' Agrate, 23, 20139

Genova 1913
Via Marostica, 4, 20146
genova1913.it

Giro di Lombardia
gazzetta.it/speciali/
girolombardia

Giro d'Italia
gazzetta.it/speciali/giroditalia

Granfondo Colnago Desenzano
granfondocolnagodesenzano.
com

Granfondo Felice Gimondi
felicegimondi.it

Masi
Velodromo Vigorelli,
Via Arona, 19, 20149
albertomasi.it
milano3v.com

Milano–Sanremo
milansanremo.co.uk

Museo del Ciclismo Madonna del Ghisallo
Via Gino Bartali, 4 22030
Magreglio
museodelghisallo.it

Olmo
Piazza Vetra, 21, 20123
olmobiciclettemilano.com

Red Hook Criterium Milano
redhookcrit.com

Rossignoli
Corso Giuseppe Garibaldi,
71, 20121
rossignoli.it

Trafiltubi
Via A. Corelli, 180,
20090 Novegro di Segrate
trafiltubi.com

Upcycle
Via Andrea Maria Ampère,
59, 20131
upcyclecafe.com

Velodromo Vigorelli
Via Arona, 19, 20149
vigorelli.org

OTHER USEFUL SITES

Eurostar
eurostar.com

Stazione di Milano Centrale
Piazza Duca D'Aosta, 1, 20124
grandistazioni.it

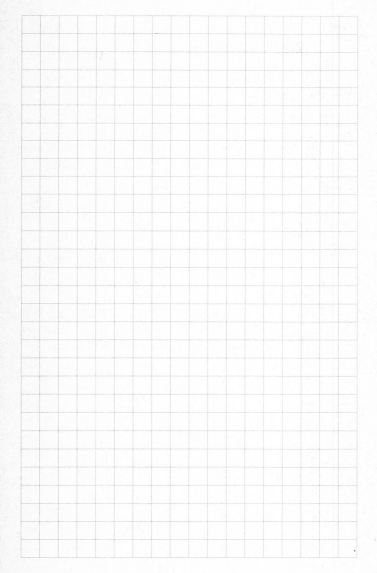

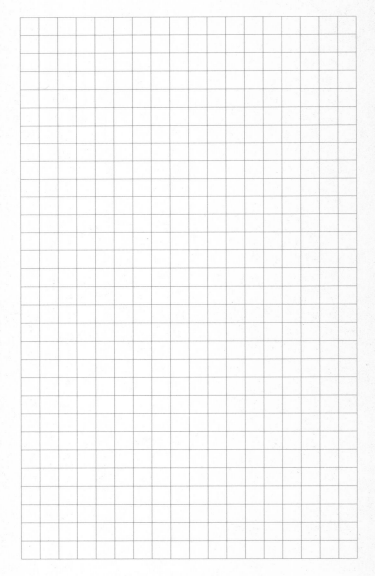

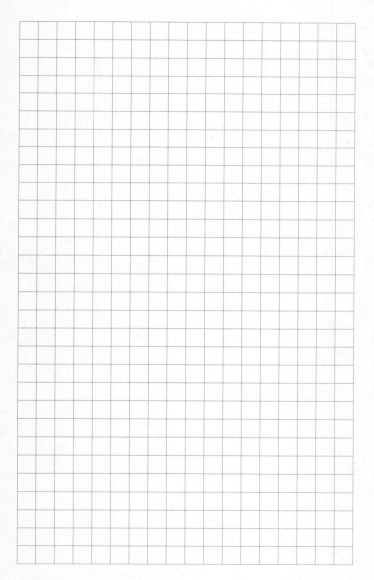

VIA GIUSEPPE PIERMANI

VIA SABOTINO BOTTICELLI
VIA GIACOMO STRADELLA
VIA GIORGIO PISANELLI

VIA FILIPPO ZANARA

VIA CARLO FORLANINI

VIA VIGILIO IRIANA
VIA ERRICO CARLOSS

VIA GIOVANNI ANTONIO AMADEO

VIA GIOVANNI ANTONIO AMADEO

S MILANO DATEO

VIALE ARGONNE

VIALE ARGONNE

VIA FRANCESCO COCCHI

VIA MASOTTO

VIA PRIVATA ANTONIO SMAREGLIA

VIA GIAN CARLO SISMONDI

VIA GIACOMO ZANELLA

VIA MONTE SUELLO
VIA LUIGI DEVOTO

CORSO 22 MARZO

PIAZZA EMILIA

VIA GIOVANNI CENA

VIA GIOVANNI BATTISTA PIRANESI

S MILANO PORTA VITTORIA

VIA MUGELLO

VIA MONTE ORTIGARA

VIA LOMBROSO

VIA COSTANZA MAGNANI

VIA CALVAIRATE

VIA PACO MUSEUM

VIA ABETONE

VIA DEGLI ETRUSCHI

VIA CADIBONA

VIA VERONESE CIMABUE

VIA DEL TURCHINO

VIA MONTE CIMONE

VIA ALBERTO CADROMCI

VIA TERTULLIANO

VIA SICILE

LANO PORTA ROMANA

VIA LEO LONGANESI

VIA PIETRO COLLETTA

VIA DIONE CASSIO

M RENTA

M CORVETTO

4 mins

½ km   ½ mile   1 km

Rapha, established in London, has always been a champion of city cycling – from testing our first prototype jackets on the backs of bike couriers, to a whole range of products designed specifically for the demands of daily life on the bike. As well as an online emporium of products, films, photography and stories, Rapha has a growing network of Cycle Clubs, locations around the globe where cyclists can enjoy live racing, food, drink and products. Rapha is also the official clothing supplier of Team Sky, the world's leading cycling team.

Rapha.